*Theories and Works
of Contemporary Architects*

Oswald Mathias Ungers
Stefan Vieths

Oswald Mathias Ungers

The Dialectic City

SKIRA
EDITORE

editor
Luca Molinari

design
Marcello Francone

translation
Francisca Garvie

Distributed outside North, Central
and South America and Italy by
Thames and Hudson Ltd., London

Contents

The Dialectic City

Cities are still being designed and built as unified systems.

The block structure has proved especially enduring and robust. Less often we find solitary buildings and ribbon developments. They are very rare. From the ancient city of Miletus to 19th-century Manhattan, there has been little real change, except in scale. The structure of a Celtic settlement differs little from that of a highly sophisticated town like St Petersburg and every atavistic linear village was built according to the same basic principles as Berne or the strenuously rational design of the modern city. The only question was whether the line ran north-south or east-west, or whether it was adapted to the topography and traffic flows.

For thousands of years, urban design has been confined to a few basic patterns, with an infinite number of formal variations. Sometimes the block is regular, as in classical antiquity and colonial times, sometimes it is more or less arbitrary, as in the Middle Ages, or monumental as in Vienna in the thirties. The basic typology remains the same, a street, lane, atrium, courtyard or square made up of blocks.

Another topos is the single or solitary building. Every archaic farm, every *kraal*, consists of single,

opposite

Basic patterns of urban design

1. Miletus
2. Manhattan
3. Neolitic settlement in Hallstadt
4. St Petersburg

adjacent buildings, arranged purely according to purpose and needs: living accommodation, storerooms, stables and ancillary buildings. The urban plan is a loose, more or less differentiated conglomerate of disparate structures. Between these lie walkways, communication lines used for various purposes, such as processions to the churches of medieval cities. Village layouts follow the same principle, complemented by public buildings such as the church, town hall or school.

Similarly, modern-day industrial estates are an accumulation, a pragmatic conglomeration of utility and industrial buildings, sometimes combined with housing and public buildings. In its basic pattern, the urban order or rather disorder resembles the empirical layout of rural settlements or historical urban settlements.

The same system of haphazard siting of solitary buildings is apparent in the arbitrary siting of highrise buildings in modern urban areas. The buildings stand alongside each other with no reference to any differentiated, overall system. They are unrelated because of the autonomous and free choice of site and their material independence.

Every period has chosen the building blocks that suited it from the basic pattern box and adapted them to its needs and ends.

This procedure would be tolerable if it was not also combined with a claim to exclusivity, to exclusive mastery of a given system. Ordered building in blocks or anarchic solitary buildings, egalitarian ribbon developments or hierarchically structured geometric forms, central or decentralized layouts are in themselves urban systems that have proved viable in the course of history and will be applied again and again in various ways in future. The problem arises when these systems are applied unchanged and exclusively, in isolation, without regard to topographical, social, economic, political or technical requirements and degenerate into ideological tools.

Modern cities are complex structures and can no longer be fitted into a single, uniform and pure system because of their complex requirements. Even during the heroic period of early modernism represented by Le Corbusier, Mies van der Rohe and Gropius, architects believed they could define and propose a binding system for a uniformly structured city. The urban developments proposed by the proponents of a new era, whether the Marxist ribbon developments of Gropius and company, the gigantic vision of Le Corbusier's "Ville radieuse," the urban ribbon developments of the Constructivists or the ecological models of Mies van der Rohe and Hilbersheimer, all failed miserably and have only passed down into the history of urban development as mutilated fragments. All these well-meant, heavily ideological endeavours can at best be understood as laboratory trials on the difficult road towards trying to put some sort of order and control into the complex problems of the city.

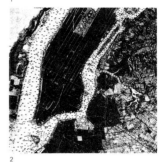

We have reached a point at which any attempt to find a complete and self-contained urban system is doomed to failure from the outset. Modernity has failed in this respect because it thinks in outdated and obsolete terms. There is no longer any question that modernity will still succeed in finding a system that suits everybody.

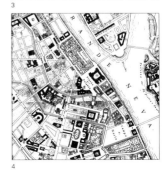

This failure is not due to any lack of effort or opportunity, but to a misguided intellectual approach. Planners argued in terms of opposites, antagonisms, old versus new, traditional versus modern, progressive versus reactionary, rather than in terms of supplementing, complementing, superimposing.

Instead of establishing links between thesis and antithesis, they opposed them and treated them separately. The failures of modern urban design are due to the exclusive focus on thesis and have led, through the total ideologization of reality, to the heterogeneous proliferations and familiar eyesores typical of the modern city. The ideology of the modern, cleaned up, tidied, standardized city, has produced just the opposite, a chaotic, confused and totally degenerate urban sprawl that nobody cares for any more because it has become totally run-down and hopelessly decayed. It is not surprising that architects have reverted to a reactionary activism and are devoting all their energies to the facades and materials of their houses, in order to forget the urban disaster they have perpetrated and to re-establish their lost role as protagonists of the environment.

The vehement debate that has recently started on the multimedia city, which is supposed to offer a new vision for the future, is no more than a continuation of the attempt to approach the urban phenomenon through technical means and to perceive the city as a uniform total work of art.

Traditional methods are transformed into new forms that fascinate the experts. The uniform city, whether multimedia or conceptual, is still regarded as the necessary objective. This multimedia chaos is nothing but a new magic formula for an old, long-obsolete ideology of the city as a totality. In their helplessness and despair, architects and even urban designers are beginning to patch together their own private urban theories. "Bricolage" is the name of the game. Some see the city of the future as a field of communication, the site of a permanent, multimedia network of communications. Stations, airports, conference centres, hotels and service areas where traffic flows meet and converge are programmed as transitory, social interfaces. Urban life only occurs in the meeting between two stops or on the multimedia Internet network, the modem or the data highway. Real contacts are replaced by an urban set menu that changes constantly and can be replaced at will. At best, urban life survives on the TV screen or the station platform. Cities are like airports, in other words, there are no cities any more. They have disintegrated into sites of more or less chance encounters. They are no longer places to stay in. Continuity is being replaced by communication. The continuous, traditional and established place is dissolving into an information system of non-committal data. The multimedia town exists outside time or space.

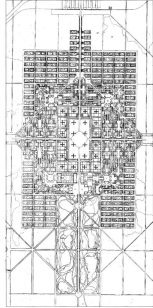

It has no history and no name and is constantly changing. Nothing lasts in the multimedia town. It reflects a boundless faith in a future of constant change, faceless and featureless. Instead of places, there are network interfaces, where information is linked up for a brief moment. The interstices in the network are equivalent and random. They are more or less close together but meaningless.

But the Piazza Navona is not a place on the Inter-

8

9

Outside the network

8. Giovanni Paolo Pannini,
*Promenade in flooded
Piazza Navona*, 1756
9. Piazza Navona, Rome

net. It is a place with its own history, which reflects continuity and in which change has taken on visible form. It is enduring. Not a multimedia mirage. It is a real, unique place to live in rather than to pass through. For cities are not in fact airports, even if they appear to be so on the Internet. They are still places whose structure and form endures.

While some seek salvation in a kind of nomadic architecture and believe that frantic improvisation is the cure-all, others lapse into a kind of historical trance and dig up old, forgotten urban concepts that have proved enduring. They rely entirely on their artistic instincts and pictorial sense. They replace sensible and rational thought by pictorial and metaphorical images. Urban space becomes a matter of subjective speculation and of the ability to create images out of fleeting ideas, that need no explanation or justification and derive purely from the experience of their inventor. This has produced astonishing works, which appeal to the tastes of the tourist and the voyeur. We are verging on a land of fantasy and totally kitsch mimicry.

The two poles of the exercises in urban concentration, the virtual city on the one hand and fantasyland on the other, are complementary strategies for escaping the current dilemma facing town planners. In actual fact they are merely hopeless attempts to cope with the chaos of the modern city. Both strategies exhaust themselves in academic shadow-boxing and inspire nobody but each other. The more the one side loses itself in visionary speculations about the future, the more deeply the other becomes entrenched in a historical morass of misunderstood models and metaphors. Neither is of any use as a complementary strategy. Neither utopia nor regression is likely to produce a viable model. These ideas are exclusive and unrealistic, quite unable to answer a single concrete question about the complex urban system. So it is as well to abandon both strategies and to leave these speculative dreams to the media experts and historians.

But any attempt to define an ideal urban design is also doomed to failure from the outset. The era of the ideal city came to an end with the late Renaissance if not before. Subsequent attempts, especially in the 19th century, to squeeze the city into an idealized straitjacket, failed largely because of industrial and social upheavals. Modern urban planners, with Italian fascism in the forefront, did not manage to create a generally valid ideal either and in the end did not make much headway with their attempts to create new towns. The same applies to the attempts after the second world war to create towns adapted to cars or ideas of social balance. It became clear that the late 20th-century city is far too heterogeneous and contradictory to be integrated in a single, however dominant plan. The contemporary town is not one but many places. It is a complex, many-layered, multifarious structure, made up of complementary and interconnected ideas, concepts and systems.

The problem of the modern city, whatever its size, is not just the centre but even more the periphery, or rather the interaction between the centre and the periphery. Paris is perhaps the most extreme example of a European city surrounded and almost strangled by a peripheral ring of *banlieues* or suburbs. Even in small and medium-sized towns, the growth of the periphery is becoming an urban plague that seems

10

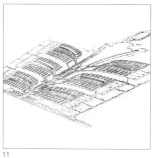
11

Failed ideal cities

10. Cancellotti, Montuori, Piccinato, Scalpelli, the New City of Sabaudia, 1933–34
11. H.B. Reichow, diagram of a neighbourhood scheme, 1948

uncontrollable. On the outskirts of the cities, industrial estates, commercial buildings and shopping malls are proliferating like cancers and traditional urban life is threatening to shift gradually towards these areas, which increasingly determine the face of today's city. This tangle of traffic routes, decentralized services, production sites, distribution centres, etc., produces a proliferation of totally inchoate structures with no aesthetic or rational meaning. At the same time the inner cities are becoming an almost insoluble economic and formal problem because of the indisputably necessary pressure to preserve their historical architectural fabric.

But the urban dilemma is not just a social, economic and technical one but above all a design problem. All urban planning is concerned mainly with bringing order into an empirical structure born of accident, practical constraints and social requirements and suggesting methods of integrating what are at times mutually exclusive urban situations into a rational system or halfway logical strategy. The planning methods applied in the past can no longer offer strategies suited to today's cities.

Unlike past attempts at standardization, we propose to describe two urban strategies that encompass the contrasts and unresolved contradictions. These strategies are based on Nikolaus van Kues' "docta de ignorantia" and concern the "coincidence of opposites," the "Coincidentia oppositorum."

this term, taken from CAD language, translates the German word Folie, which means a thin sheet or film, usually transparent, and in this case signifies a background on which something is superimposed. This reflects the idea of the city as a basis for successive layers of planning.

The two strategies are as follows:
1. The strategy of complementary places.
2. The strategy of the city as layer.*

18

Unlike the village, the small city or the ideal city, today's big city is no longer uniform. It is a heterogeneous amalgam of different elements, systems and functions. The big city reaches out into the regions and is a fragmentary and open structure that can no longer be integrated within a coherent system because of the varied, self-contradictory requirements imposed on it.

The modern city is dialectical, it is both thesis and antithesis. It reflects the contradictions of society and also its technical systems. It is no longer possible to find unified forms or consistent solutions which still incorporate everything in a single system as in the historical city up to the 19th century. The idea of the city as a comprehensive unit has become increasingly evanescent in the course of history and what has remained is a confused, almost uncontrollable apparatus that tends towards increasingly large excrescences, perversions and dissolution. The individual, nameable places play an important part in this trend towards the dissolution of the city centre. Rather than being a unified concept, the city is now a structure made up of "complementary places." The many contrasting areas, areas of recreation, culture, commerce, residence and work, together form a loose urban association. The modern city shaped by technology and cultural demands is made up not of a total jumble, but of a system of mutually complementary, significant places. That is why an appropriate method must be found of identifying the character of these very disparate places, defining it and developing its specific features, either by adding the functions that are lacking or by perfecting existing ones.

12

13

14

15

The city made up of "complementary places" consists of the largest possible variety of different parts, in each of which a special urban aspect is developed with a view to the whole. In a sense it is a system of the "city within the city." Every part has its own special features, without however being complete and self-contained. In each case only one aspect, residential, cultural or commercial, is highly developed and therefore combines with other highly developed places to form a complex system, a kind of federation. Examples of complementary places are the historical city, but also the new settlements on the periphery, whether industrial estates or large recreational areas. The places are structured hierarchically. Some are more, others less important. Their value derives from the place itself and not from any idealized concept of it. That is why in principle any form of building, highrise or low-level, large-scale or solitary, is possible.

The structural forms are not exclusive but inclusive, varied and as heterogeneous as possible. The aim is variety rather than uniformity. Contradictions, conflicts are part of the system and remain unresolved. The aim is not to resolve them but to demarcate them clearly and unambiguously. Every part, every place primarily exists for itself and only evolves in its complementary relationship with another, self-contained place. The places are like autonomous entities, like small microcosms, independent worlds, with their own special features, advantages and disadvantages, integrated in a larger, urban macrocosm, a metropolis and landscape made up of these small worlds.

The art of urban design consists in identifying the places within the urban chaos, naming them and discovering their special features. So urban design is the art of discovery and not invention. No new systems —technical or otherwise—are added. What exists through chance, necessity, inadequacy, is accepted and regarded as a layer. The various existing elements and parts and fragments are used to build and develop a new urban structure with its own areas and places. The city made up of complementary places is open and can be interpreted, it is both mixed and adaptable, useful, non-ideological and unpretentious, open to innovation while also preserving the past.

The second concept used for structuring and ordering the modern-day city is "the city as layer." Cities consist of series of superimposed layers, either complementary or diametrically opposed. The various systems, whether transport, supplies and services, parks, water, buildings, are regarded individually, as part of the complex urban structure. They can be isolated and therefore become available for use and operational. They can be supplemented, reduced, perfected or changed. Each individual system influences, modifies or changes the next. The superimposition of the existing, with its pressures and needs, modifies the ideal structural concept and this produces fragmentary structures. Even such self-important technical systems as the 19th-century railway networks that burst into the city like hurricanes could still be constructed in an ideal form. It was merely modified and adapted by topographical and historical factors. This gave rise to contradictions and problems of adaptation that led to unique, unpredictable results. They transformed the city into a continuum of unresolved, mutual conflicts. Conflicts, fragments, unresolved contradictions and

opposite

The modern city

12. Rostock-Reutershagen
13. Humboldt harbour, Berlin
14. Neuss suburbs
15. Spreeinsel, Berlin

21

16

17

18

The city as a sum of complementary places

16. Berlin
17. Edinburgh
18. Wiesbaden

oppositions are, however, the characteristic criterion of the "town as layer." The various structures are superimposed, like the layers of a historical city.

The method consists of overlaying each new and more complete system with another layer, monitoring and considering the effects and exploiting the creative results. Urban design thus shifts from being a purely emotional process to becoming a rational procedure, in which every decision, every further degree of complexity can be monitored and comprehended. The individual layers can be evaluated and emphasized depending on the priorities. This frees urban design from the usual desire to improve, based purely on feeling and sudden inspiration. The art is to classify properly and to identify and evaluate the reciprocal effect of the superimposed systems. Rational decision-making takes the place of subjective feeling.

The strategy of "the city as layer," which can be regarded as a structural approach that complements the morphological approach of the "city as complementary places," obviously presupposes looking at the city as a complex whole and considering the present-day city in practical terms. Only if the city is seen as a whole do the tensions and oppositions that lead to its disparate variety and complexity become apparent. The unfinished, if you like provisional nature of the city is both the basis and the object of urban planning. The variety of forms and spaces is intentional, the result of a clear and strictly defined process. This process takes account of topographical and historical factors, of technical procedures as well as social requirements and formal concepts. Nothing is decided in advance; decisions are taken on a case by case basis.

The "city as layer" approach to planning aims to create an instrument and a vocabulary for transforming the chaotic conglomerate of the modern-day city into an orderly, comprehensible structure while retaining, and if possible even increasing, its high level of complexity. This method is also designed to emphasize the discursive nature of the city, so that urban development can be guided into and follow orderly planning lines, based on hypotheses that are examined experimentally.

19

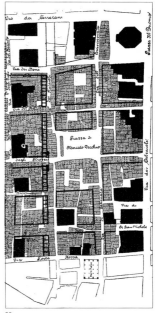

20

The city as superimposed layers

19. Trier: topography, Roman city, medieval city
20. Florence: medieval city, renaissance city
21. Rome: Roman city, medieval city, baroque city

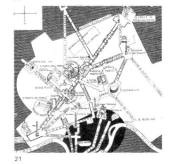

21

23

Projects 1991–95

Introduction

Below we describe eight projects designed as competition pieces in recent years.

These projects document the application of the strategies described above to actual projects and show the potential of this kind of working method.

They are divided into two groups. The first comprises projects based on the concept of complementary places:

– Euroforum, Cologne, 1992
– Royal Porcelain Factory (Königliche
    Porzellanmanufaktur - KPM), Berlin, 1993
– Cathedral Square, Magdeburg, 1993
– Humboldt Colonnades, Berlin, 1995

The strategy of the city as layer is represented by the second group of projects:

– Rostock-Reutershagen, 1995
– Spreeinsel, Berlin, 1994
– Neuss-Hammfeld, 1994
– Potsdamer Platz and Leipziger Platz, 1991

In the case of both groups, the specifications and

Complementary places

1. Royal Porcelain Factory, Berlin, 1993
2. Magdeburg Cathedral Square, 1993

scale of the projects differed widely, from rebuilding an urban block (KPM, Berlin) to planning a complex city as in Neuss.

The same applies to the nature of the urban design areas: from anonymous areas on the outskirts of city, as in Rostock and Cologne, to historical sites of prime importance such as Magdeburg Cathedral Square and Spreeinsel in Berlin.

The very diversity of the projects shows that the urban strategies we have described can offer only a rough framework within which different themes, corresponding to concrete conditions, are developed for the individual projects.

For instance, in the case of the project for Magdeburg Cathedral Square, the main emphasis is on the historical dimension of the area, while the project for the Humboldt Colonnades in Berlin centres on existing urban transport structures—the station and Humboldt harbour.

The wide range of different themes reflects the different levels of complexity in the planning: while the project for Rostock-Reutershagen, for instance, represents a very elementary application, reduced to just a very few parameters, of the principle of the city as layer, the project for Potsdam Square and Leipzig Square in Berlin is extremely complex and ambiguous because of the many superimposed layers.

The open and experimental nature of the approaches is reflected in the differentiated way the urban strategies are applied.

Each project is perceived in an experimental manner and requires a specific interpretation of the chosen strategy, that is, the methods, initially defined in abstract terms, undergo a constant process of refinement, differentiation and development. This can produce multiform, undogmatic and very complex urban structures, in spite of the strictly rational planning process.

3

4

The city as layer

3. Neuss-Hammfeld, 1994
4. Potsdamer Platz
and Leipziger Platz, Berlin, 1991

Complementary Places

1992
Euroforum, Cologne

A typical commission: to transform an industrial sector near the city centre into a new urban district providing services, housing and small industry. The surface area is large in this case, and plays an important part in the urban structure of Cologne because of its location. Situated directly on the Rhine, it is intersected by the approach to the Zoo bridge and thus forms one of the main accesses to the city centre. The urban environment around this area contrasts sharply with the centre of Cologne. It features large industrial estates and transport infrastructure, side by side with residential areas and exhibition buildings. Here the context of the traditional city dissolves in a patchwork of large urban structures each obeying its own laws.

The New District
The design for the Cologne Euroforum is an elementary application of the principle of complementary places. The specific problem was how to define an urban place "per se," that could survive in the existing chaos, in this inchoate townscape. The design strategy was therefore to give the new district its own spatial structure and identity. As in the planning of new cities,

Euroforum, Cologne

1–3. Approaches to the projected motorway area. In the background the Cathedral of Cologne

a clearly defined structure is established by means of a strict grid of blocks, which is further differentiated in terms of urban space and function. That means that the existing urban structures were not developed further but were complemented by a new, autonomous urban development area.

Accordingly, we designed an orthogonal system of urban blocks, adapted to the existing highrise buildings. The initial standard size of the building block is 41×41 metres, which is then varied according to the features of the site and the requirements of the programme. This produces a district with its own geometry and precise, clearly defined spaces. At the same time, the plan is flexible enough to be able to integrate the buildings worth preserving without difficulty. A large park in front of the highrise building acts as the spatial centre of the Euroforum.

Typology of Blocks and Spaces

The further structural and spatial development of the area is based on a system of blocks and streets. There is a variety of different types of block, depending on its function and location within the area, for instance a four-part block, a terraced block, a block containing objects, a double block, etc. This produces a varied structural typology that reflects the urban atmosphere of the district.

Like the different types of buildings, the different functions of the streets produce a typology of street spaces, which, together with the central park, creates a varied spatial structure. As a result of this differentiation, the rational, strict basic system produces a complex urban structure.

The Entrance to the City

The real urban significance of the new district is reflected by a highrise gateway spanning the urban motorway. In the general urban context, it designates the entrance to the city and relates this new urban area to existing central areas of the city with their dominant features, such as the university district or the old city and cathedral.

4

5

6

The entrance to the city

4. Porta Nigra, Trier
5. Giovanni Battista Piranesi, *Trajan arch in Ancona*
6. El Lissitsky: project for a skyscraper (*Der Wolkenbügel*), Moscow, 1923

7–8. Vertical section,
view from the south-east

9. Axonometry

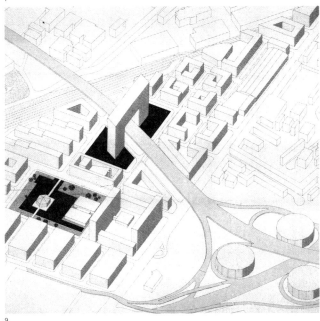

11–12. Vertical section,
view from the south-west

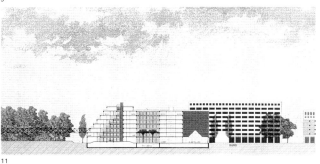

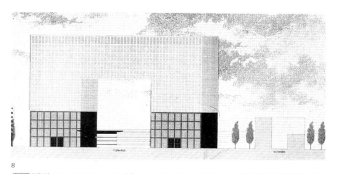

8

10. General planimetry

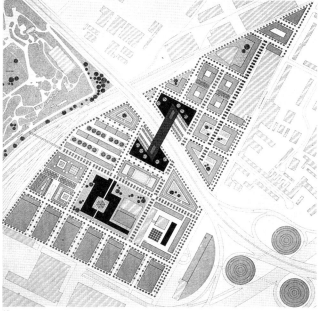

10

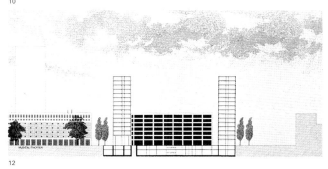

12

37

13. Planimetry
of the standard plan

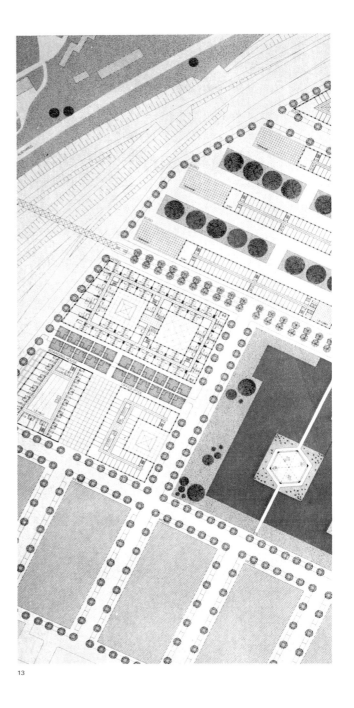

13

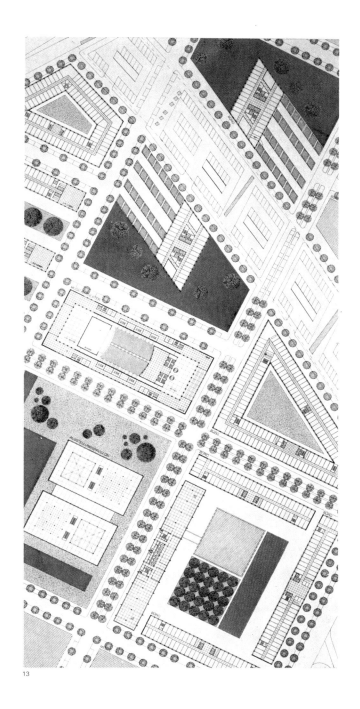

13

1993
Royal Porcelain Factory (KPM), Berlin

The need to redevelop the Berlin KPM with its wealth of tradition arose from the decision to abandon most of the production in this inner-city site and to convert the area to other uses. While retaining the most historic part of the building, a comprehensive plan was required for the construction of various university and commercial buildings and for an imposing new KPM administrative building.

Within the urban structure of Berlin, the KPM site is located at a central intersection; it is on the Strasse des 17. Juni—the main urban axis in Berlin, which is crossed by the suburban railway at this point—and situated between the built-up Charlottenburg area and the rural expanse of the zoo. Its position by a road and an intersection is reflected by the morphology of the existing buildings. Buildings of different types, intended for different uses and purposes, stand closely adjacent. First there are the KPM production sites—including the historic 18th-century factories—then there are a whole range of different types of housing, a university institute dating from the seventies and finally, right on the Strasse des 17. Juni, the Ernst-Reuter-Haus, a typically imposing turn-of-the-century administrative

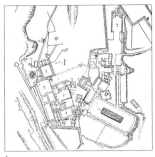

Design made up of solitary buildings 1

1. Villa Adriana, Tivoli, detail of the general planimetry
2. Villa Adriana, Tivoli, detail of the model

building. Some of these fragments are of high quality and each of them reflects a specific concept of urban building and therefore of the history of Berlin.

A Design Made Up of Solitary Buildings

The proposed plan accepts the fragmentary and contradictory nature of the buildings and takes it as a theme: instead of turning the area into a unifying, orthogonal system of blocks and streets, the haphazard nature of the existing structures is taken as the basis for an urban design made up of solitary buildings.

During this process of transformation, structures born of chance are integrated in a rational composition and existing urban fragments become part of a collage of complementary structures and form a campus of solitary buildings. The microcosm of this urban block is an almost ideal transposition of the principle of complementary places. The project allows the original building tradition to continue without interruption, by preserving most of the existing structures and transposing them into a new overall plan. It also allows for very varied types of building, in line with their various uses. At the same time, it creates a typology of clearly-defined external spaces, ranging from the garden to the courtyard and the campus.

Elements of the Design

The urban design is made up of the following solitary buildings, each of which represents a specific type:

– the KPM tower: at the entrance to the zoo, a significant urban feature, we proposed a tower which, together with the tower of L. Leo's research institute on the other side of the Strasse des 17. Juni, forms an urban gateway. The reference to the Ernst-Reuter-Haus is created by a base supporting two different types of building: the slender office tower and the compact cube of the firing room.

– the hippodrome: we proposed a building complex, which encompasses the historical, U-shaped KPM building, made up of a long, hippodrome-like inner courtyard containing the senate library and the art school

– the Ernst-Reuter-Haus: the impressive double court-yard is complemented by extensions also used as offices

– the double square: the block bordering the Siegmunds Hof is supplemented by a second angled block to form a courtyard

– the double slab: the eight-storey slab is supplemented by a second slab to form an H-shaped complex

– the city houses: west of the hippodrome we planned six city houses, mainly for residential purposes. They complete the design on the side bounded by the Englische Strasse.

3

4

Design made up of solitary buildings 2

3. Rome in the imperial age, detail of the general planimetry
4. Rome in the imperial age, detail of the model

5. View from Reuter-Platz

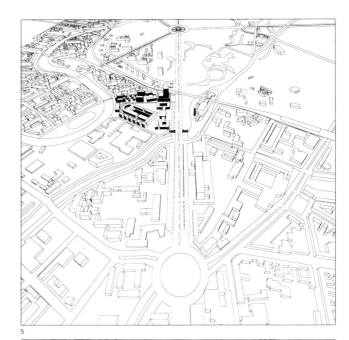

5

6. View from
Charlottenburger Tor

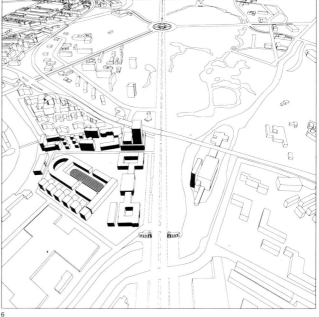

6

44

7. Structure of built area
8. Structure of spaces

9. General planimetry

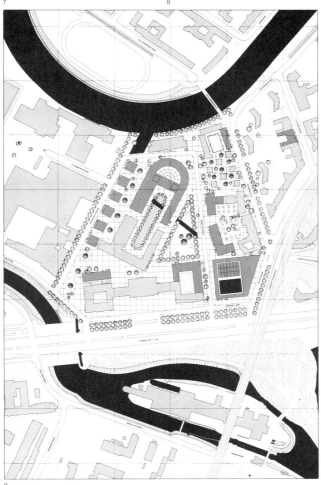

45

10. Section of the Senate Library,
Academy of Arts

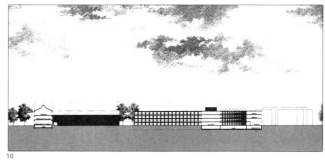

10

11. Planimetry
of the ground floor

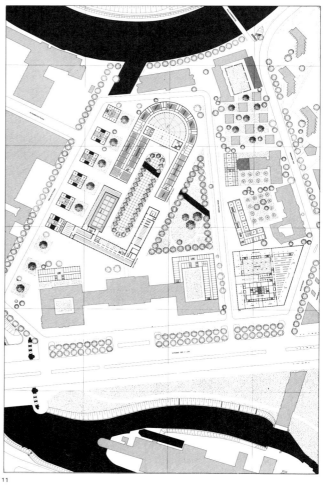

11

12. View from the south

12

13. View from
Charlottenburger Tor

13

47

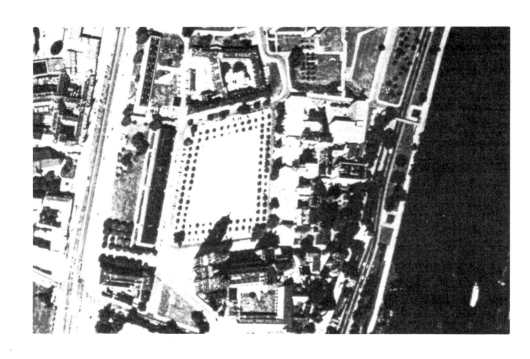

1993
Magdeburg Cathedral Square

The urban environment of Magdeburg Cathedral is now in a state that crassly contradicts the cultural and historical importance of the site. Many of the existing buildings bear no relation to one another and have little spatial significance, so that the urban fabric dissolves into wide, unstructured spaces which take on an almost rural aspect. The variety and quality of the existing urban fragments contrast with the desolate, general urban framework. There are very important cultural and historical buildings, such as the cathedral and the convent Unserer lieben Frauen (Our Dear Ladies). But there are also a wide variety of types of secular residential and commercial buildings. Common to all of them is that they represent prototype basic elements of different urban models: they refer back to the medieval and baroque city, to the 19th-century city and to the city during the post-war period of reconstruction.

Design
In planning Magdeburg Cathedral Square, priority was given to its historical importance and the surviving buildings. The strategy of complementary places was

Types of building

1. Rome, 1748
(detail of Nolli's plan)
2. Le Corbusier, Plan Voisin,
Paris, 1922 (detail)

applied in almost exemplary fashion here: starting from the existing fragments, we began by identifying three urban design areas, each of which represents a particular urban type:
– the cathedral district
– the residential area round Our Dear Ladies' convent
– and the original buildings south of the cathedral.
Each of these structures is marked by a specific type of building and spatial definition. In a second stage, they were supplemented by new buildings adapted to the respective spatial and block typology. This has created three districts each with its own, different identity and each organized round its own spatial centre.

The cathedral district: the central district of the competition area was supplemented in such a way as to clearly demarcate the square again and complete the large-scale building complex down to the Elbe. The new structures have the same "poché" block design as the existing buildings.

Residential area round Our Dear Ladies' convent: the open, ribbon-like housing from the reconstruction period was converted into meander blocks and continued down to the Fürstenwall. The spatial centre of the district is formed by a sculpture park which also encompasses the existing convent building as though it were another object. The new structures contain housing and, on the ground floor, shops and restaurants.

Original buildings on the Materlik area: south of the cathedral square, the 19th-century extension of the city with its orthogonal street grid and scattered perimeter blocks is still clearly identifiable. Here, we only intervened in order to complete the blocks and to remove the viaduct in the Leibnitzstrasse/Danzstrasse area.

In analogy to these three districts, we proposed another type of block for the central inner city area along the Ernst-Reuter-Allee, designed for very dense shop and office use.

These urban building blocks are linked by a complete street network and by the spatial interrelationship between the three central green areas. Moreover, they have a view of the Elbe in common, thanks to the extended rampart walkway, which is reminiscent of the Dresden terraces overlooking the Elbe, and underlines the special cultural and urban significance of the entire complex.

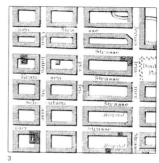

3

4

3. Friedrichstadt, Berlin, 1833
4. Bernardo Bellotto (1720–80),
*Dresden terraces overlooking
the Elbe*

51

5. View from the south

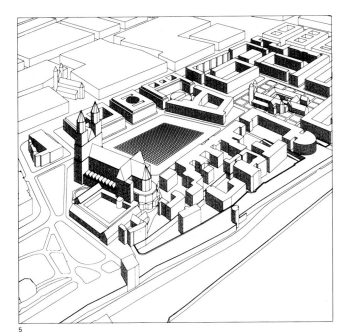

5

6. View from the east

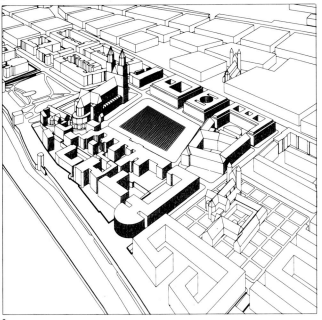

6

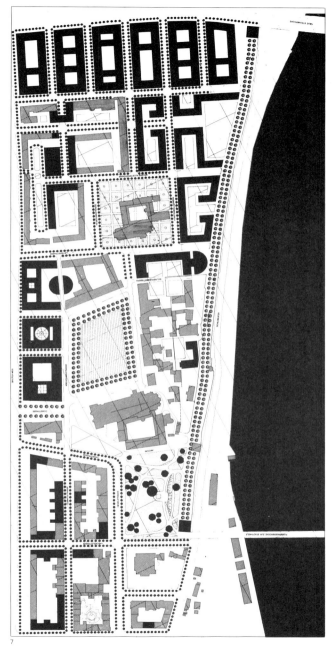

7. General planimetry

53

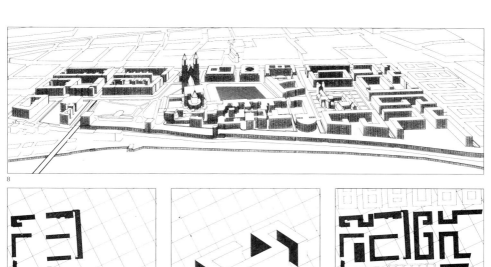

8

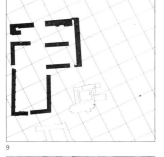

9

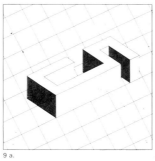

9 a.

9 b.

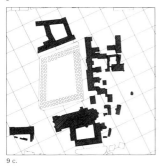

9 c.

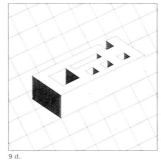

9 d.

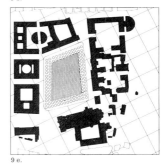

9 e.

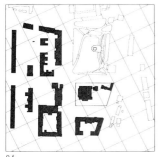

9 f.

9 g.

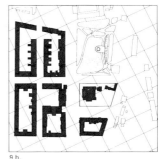

9 h.

55

10. Planimetry
of the ground floor

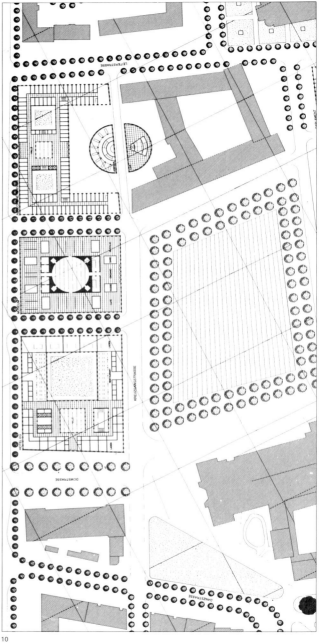

10

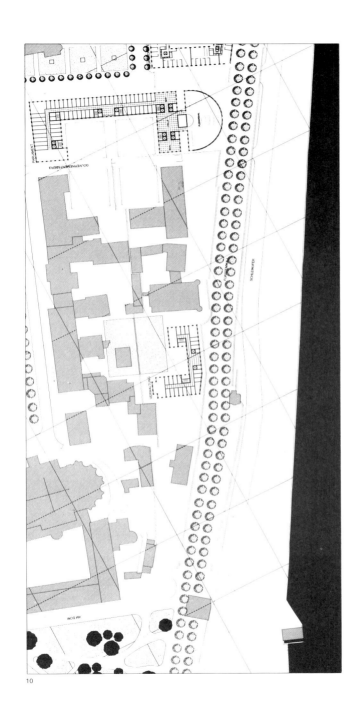

11–12. View from the Elbe

13. View, plan of the hotel

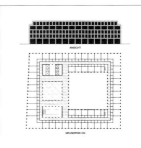

15. Structure of the built area

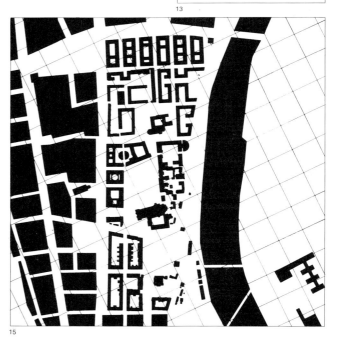

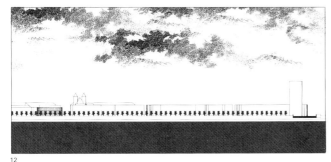

12

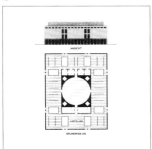

14

14. View, plan of the museum

16. Structure of spaces

16

59

1995
Humboldt Colonnades, Berlin

The competition area for the redesigned Lehrter Station district forms the northern boundary of the zoo in the Spreebogen district. So it is very close to the Reichstag and the future government district.

At present, the area is largely undeveloped and characterized by the waters of the Spree river and Humboldt harbour, whose strictly geometric design harks back to Lenne's plans in the 19th century.

The new Lehrter Station is to be built on this site in the next few years; its favourable location gives it a central part to play in Berlin's transport planning. At the time of the competition, the plans for the station were so advanced that its location and architectural form had already been defined and were as much a part of the terms of the competition as the related urban railway infrastructure.

Against this backdrop, the competition set two main tasks:

– To integrate the large-scale transport infrastructure and the existing station plans within a new district.
– To define the Spreebogen and Humboldt harbour in terms of the general urban space.

Basic urban design

1. Lenne's urban design
2. Traffic plan

General Urban Design

The basic urban design follows on from Lenne's urban plan for the Spreebogen and aims to turn the Humboldt harbour into a meaningful urban space.

The main existing urban design elements are the semi-circular Spreebogen and the axially related form of the shipping canal and Humboldt harbour. In addition there is the planned linear block of government buildings, which, like the solitary buildings of the Reichstag and Bundesrat, make a reference to the north-south axis that runs straight through Humboldt harbour.

In order to complete this large-scale structural complex properly in the north, it is proposed to give a structural framework to Humboldt harbour in the form of colonnades. In this way the very beautiful structure of Humboldt harbour, which is scarcely perceptible at present, acquires the quality of a unique urban space.

The colonnades are flanked by two open spaces: to the east they adjoin a park connecting the Charité with the Spree, to the west is the station forecourt. The station building is supplemented by two other solitary buildings—a highrise office block and a hotel cube—so that it is incorporated in a composition of three object-buildings and forms part of an urban system.

The western boundary of the station square consists of a compact block structure of office buildings. In line with the strategy of "complementary places," this creates three "strips" of different urban structures, stretching from the Invalidenstrasse to the Spree:

– the colonnades, whose structure responds directly

to the quality of this particular area. It makes a reference to similar urban, waterside buildings, such as the Alster arcades in Hamburg

– the composition of urban object-buildings—bridge, cube, slab—which is derived from the particular features of the station design and is adapted to such situations as the "Gendarmenmarkt" in Friedrichstadt

– the compact urban block structure, typical of the required commercial and office blocks. In its dimensions it resembles the structure of Berlin's Friedrichstadt.

The Humboldt Colonnades

Framing Humboldt harbour with colonnades creates an urban space whose imposing form is a reference to the Berlin tradition of large, geometric squares, such as Leipziger Platz, Pariser Platz and Mehrring Platz.

Like these squares, the Humboldt Colonnades mark the place of arrival, in this case for travellers arriving at Lehrter Station, whose glass-roofed platforms cross through the Humboldt Colonnades.

In terms of typology, the building forms a continuous "wall." It is broken in many places and dissolves into rows of colonnades at significant urban places. This creates a number of links between Humboldt harbour and the surrounding urban spaces. The longitudinal line of colonnades sometimes follows the contours of the harbour directly and is sometimes set back, creating an interchange of colonnaded areas and open spaces by the water. A promenade runs directly along the shore, on the same level as the former wharf. The variety of spatial structures is matched by the variety of uses. There are restaurants,

3

4

5

Design of the squares

3. Leipziger Platz
4. Pariser Platz
5. Mehrring Platz
(Belle Alliance-Platz)

cafés and shops on the lower floors, while the upper floors are intended for housing and hotels.

Station Square

The design of the station square as an open space with objects placed within it allows for an optimal spatial link both with the main traffic axis of the Invalidenstrasse to the north and with the zoo and the adjacent government district to the south.

The highrise slab in the north marks the position of the station along the Invalidenstrasse. Looking towards the government district, the hotel cube accentuates the spatial transition from the station to the large open space of the zoo. Here the composition of the objects—slab, bridge, cube—shows to full advantage.

Together, the station square and the Humboldt Colonnades form a double square of two antagonistic urban spaces. Like the double square of the Leipziger Platz/Potsdamer Platz, this creates an impressive spatial composition made up of a quiet, self-contained square by the water and an open, lively traffic square.

As in Magdeburg, here too the principle of the city as the sum of individual places emerges very clearly. In this case, however, the various urban designs are not derived from historical building fragments but from the interplay with the urban infrastructure, the various transport facilities and Humboldt harbour.

Waterside urban spaces

6. Lisbon, Praça do Commercio
7. Giovanni Battista Piazzetta
(1683–1754), *Venice*
8. Telford, Hardwick, project
for St Catherine's Docks,
London, 1825

9. View of the station square

9

10. Humboldt harbour

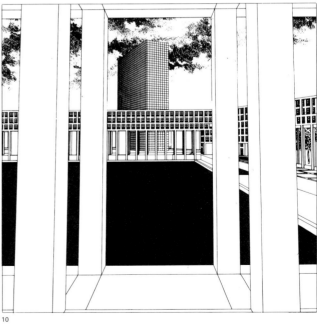

10

66

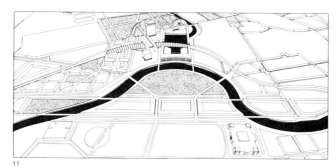

11. View of the zoo

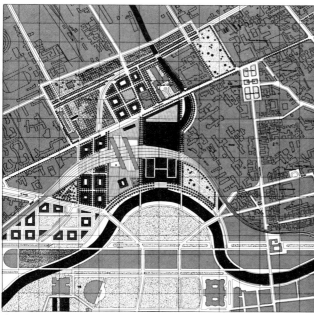

12. General planimetry

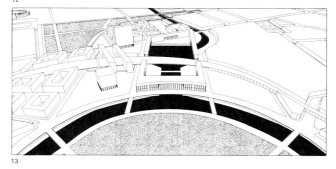

13. View from the Spreebogen

67

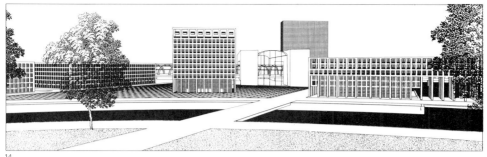

14

15

16

17

15 a.

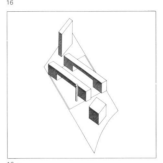

16 a.

17 a.

15 b.

16 b.

17 b.

69

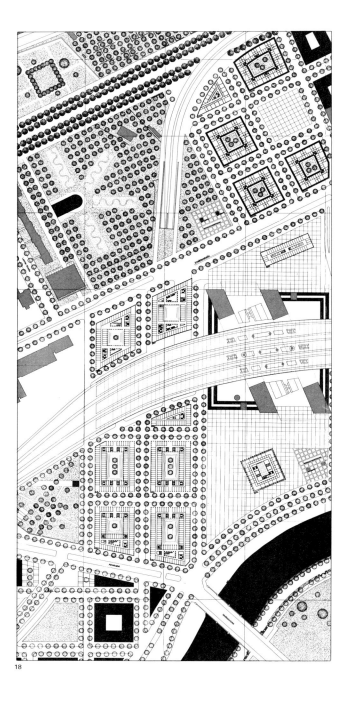

18

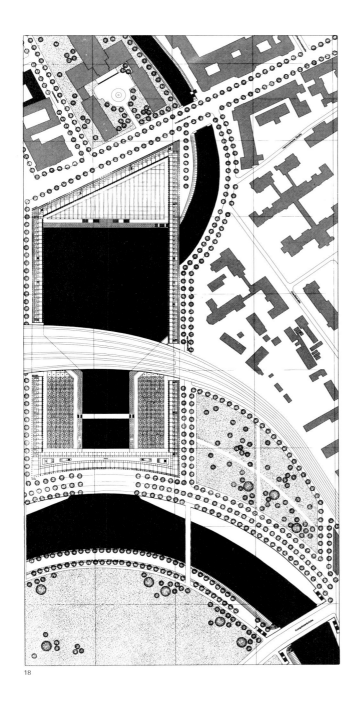

19–20. View from the Spree

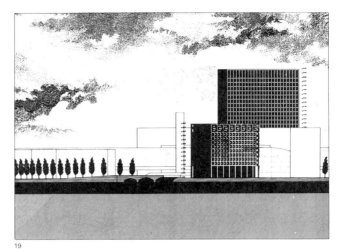

19

21. The square seen from
the riverside

21

23–24. Vertical sections

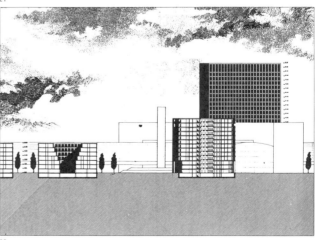

23

20

22. Shipping canal

22

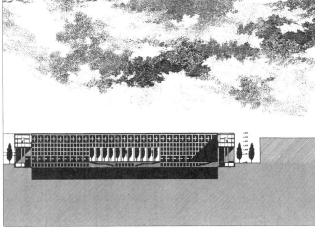

24

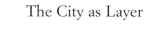

The City as Layer

1995
Rostock-Reutershagen

The competition area comprises the central area of Reutershagen. This northern district of Rostock was largely constructed in the years following the second world war and its structure is based on the modernist urban design of our times with its object-like structures and loosely defined urban spaces. This applies in particular to the city centre under consideration here, which is basically an undeveloped area with a few temporary buildings.

The project for Rostock is a very simple and basic application of the concept of the "city as layer." An "urban mass" of clearly defined form is planted in the "empty centre" of the existing building structure. Superimposing the existing road network on this urban mass produces a system of urban spaces. This creates an urban structure analogous to that of Rostock. The proposed compact urban development acquires the same function for Reutershagen as the city centre of Rostock does for the city as a whole: it represents the heart of urban life.

Like the historic inner city, the new city centre of Reutershagen is an independent urban unit that is easy to understand and whose autonomy is emphasized by

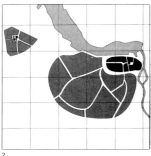

Analogy between the city and its centre (Gesamtstadt)

1. Historic inner city, Rostock
2. Rostock and Reutershagen, with their historic city centres

the clear basic design. As in the inner city, the buildings are mainly compact and, in this case, of six storeys, into which clearly-defined urban spaces are, as it were, incised. These spaces are clearly distinct from the open, fluid spaces of the existing structures. The dense, urban quality of the proposed buildings is also emphasized by the choice of a uniform material (clinker brick).

The city centre is divided into four blocks by a crossroads, based on the existing road plan. Within these four blocks are two squares. The market square acts as the spatial centre of public life in Reutershagen in terms of its functions but also its proportions and treatment (arcades, surfacing of the square, plants). A second square is situated on the axis of the Ulrich-von-Hutten-Strasse, forming the spatial entrance to the city centre. This square is designed as an ornamental and traffic area, intended mainly for prestige with its areas of water.

As a result of these measures, the autonomous form of the city centre is manipulated on a second, creative level, so that the new plan subtly refers back to the existing structures. So the original buildings and the new plan are not unrelated to each other but complementary and contrasting.

3

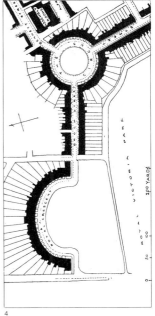

4

Urban designs

3. Lucca, the market square
4–5. Bath, "The Royal Crescent"
and "The Circus"

5

79

6. View from the Ulrich-von-Hutten-Strasse

7. Analogies between the historic centres

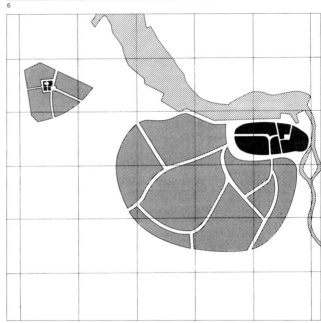

8. Structure of the built area
9. Project for the green spaces

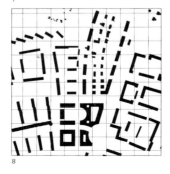
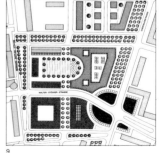

10. View of the market square

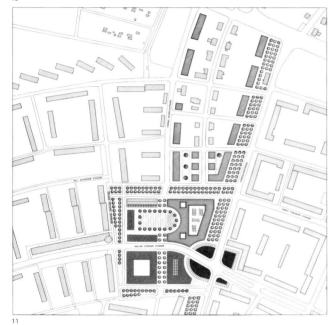

11. General planimetry

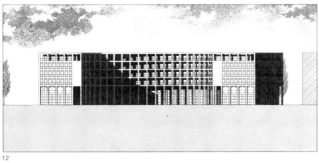

12. View from the market square

81

13. Planimetry
of the standard plan

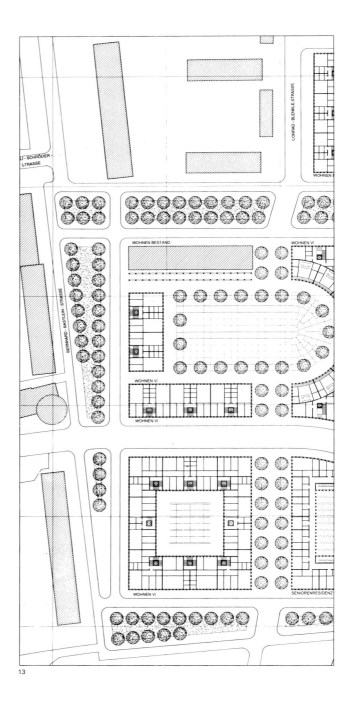

13

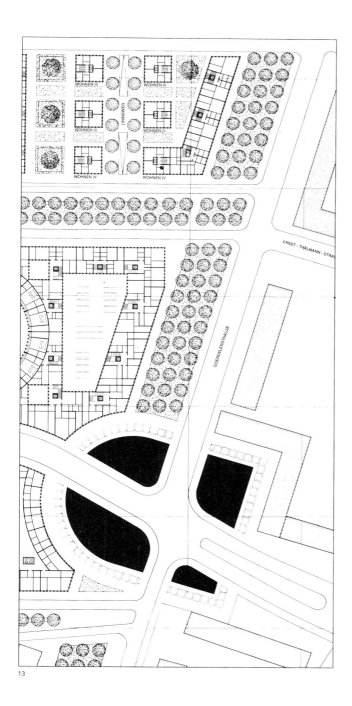

13

1994
Spreeinsel, Berlin

Spreeinsel forms an important part of the historic centre of Berlin and accordingly has a varied past. First it was the site of one of the earliest core settlements of the city, later it became the palace of the Prussian kings and finally, as the cornerstone of a humanist "Spree Athens," it became the site of some of Schinkel's most important buildings: the Friedrichwerder church, the Building Academy and the Old Museum. After the second world war, Spreeinsel became the site of major state events for the newly formed GDR: the partially destroyed castle was pulled down and replaced by the poorly proportioned Marx-Engels-Platz and the "Palace of the Republic."

Against this background the real problem of the competition project becomes clear; aside from the urban redevelopment of the desolate site it raises the question of how to treat its history and monuments. In the run-up to the competition, this question provoked vehement public debate about the demolition of the Palace of the Republic and the reconstruction of the historic castle.

The terms of the competition stipulate that, out of respect for history, the Palace of the Republic may not

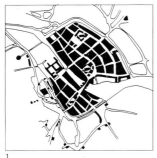

*Urban development
of the Spreeinsel*

1. 1650
2. 1850
3. 1990

be pulled down nor may the castle be reconstructed. Instead, the palace was to be preserved as a monument. On the basis of this decision, an attempt should be made, however, to take due account of the monumental nature of the palace. It was no longer to be a show-piece but to be integrated in a self-contained urban space. This is achieved by treating the building not as a solitary structure but as part of a street block and integrating it into the fabric of the city.

Following this line of thought, the street block construction is continued logically up to the "Unter den Linden" street, where, together with the front of the palace, it forms a self-contained backdrop to the "Lustgarten" or pleasance. This achieves two objects: firstly, the dense network of buildings on Spreeinsel continues up to this boundary line; secondly, the pleasance is placed within a spatial frame that incorporates the solitary buildings of the cathedral, the Old Museum and the "Zeughaus" (arsenal).

But since for reasons of history the site of the former castle cannot be built on, the ground plan of the castle is omitted from the block structure. This creates a negative space on the site of the castle. In the ground plan the castle area is an open space, surrounded on every side by buildings, which can be used as a historic park, although only fragmentarily at present.

The fusion of two historically mutually contradictory ideologies into a unified urban space would not only reveal the course of history but would still work if the pro-demolition supporters won. For even assuming that for whatever reasons the palace had to be demolished, while on the other hand the castle could not be reconstructed for ethical or other reasons, the concept of a negative space would still remain valid. The open space in the form of the ground plan of the castle would remain separate from the dense urban architecture and serve as a historic park. Preserving it as a memorial space would bring the history of the city alive again.

The urban design for the Spreeinsel is based on the plan of Berlin designed by Schinkel, namely solitary buildings incorporated in the general structure of the city. In his 1851 plan, Schinkel enhanced the general ground plan of the city by careful additions and created a varied play between architectural highpoints and general roadside buildings. The proposed plan for Spreeinsel follows the same lines. Solitary buildings such as Friedrichwerder church, the Council of State building, together with the proposed restoration of the Military Command, the Building Academy, the Old Mint, the plinth for the William I memorial and a few architectural jewels within the block form the spatial and architectural highpoints of what is otherwise a more or less secular urban structure.

The existing buildings are integrated to form compact blocks of buildings, creating a well-defined system of public roads, perimeter blocks and green courtyards.

Together with the Council of State, the Foreign Ministry forms a varied block that includes inner courtyards, squares and walkways. The existing structure of the old Reichsbank building houses the Ministry of the Interior. An entrance block with an internal passage forms the link with the Werdersche market. The Old Mint designed by Gentz could be restored within this complex and used as a reception building.

4

5

The building as an object and a negative space

4. Berlin castle, 1916
5. Place Royale, Paris
(now Place des Vosges, detail of Turgot's project, 1734–35)

opposite

Solitary buildings and urban structures, Schinkel's buildings in the Spreeinsel area

6. Friedrichwerder church
7. The Building Academy
8. The Old Museum
9. The New Guard-House

The character of the old Werdersche market should be restored. Besides the church, the reconstruction of the Building Academy, which could be used as a library of American memorabilia, would be an important means of achieving this. The old block buildings could be integrated here too and used as a conference centre. The buildings on the Werdersche market are rounded off by the Media Centre block, which also forms the boundary of the green area. The buildings around the future castle square should serve a wide variety of urban functions: shops and cultural facilities on the ground level of the square, arcades, offices and practices on the next floor and housing above that.

The plan is not an attempt to redesign the centre of Berlin or to replace existing buildings and structures with new ones or to restore old structures, but instead to complete the fragmentary and contradictory existing buildings with careful additions and supplements to form a stratified, varied urban system. The strategy of the city as layer is applied here in a subtle, not very explicit way: it gives priority to the differentiated and flexible handling of the individual historical monuments and the different urban areas. That is why the proposed structure is not uniform and exclusive but dialectical and differentiated.

6

7

8

9

10. View from the south-west.
First planning stage

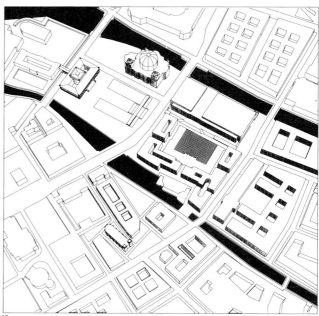

10

11. View from the south-west.
Second planning stage

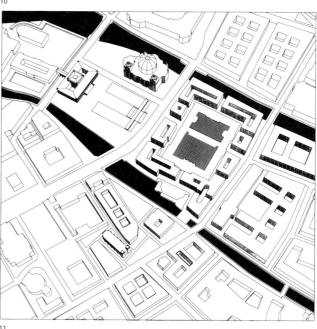

11

90

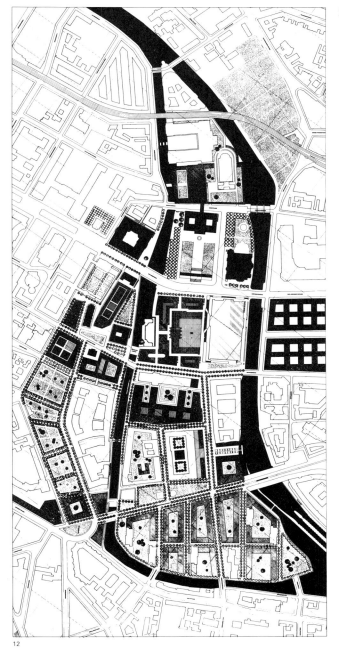

12

13–14. View of Breite Strasse
and Luststrasse

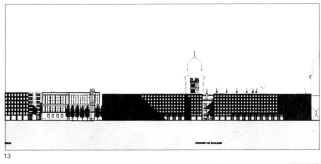

13

15. Schinkel's plan

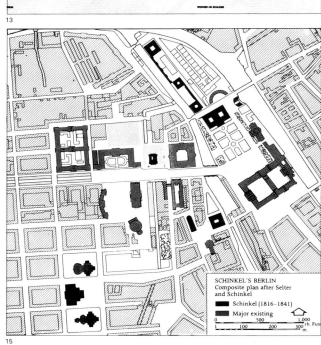

SCHINKEL'S BERLIN
Composite plan after Selter
and Schinkel

■ Schinkel (1816–1841)

■ Major existing

15

17–18. View of the Spreekanal

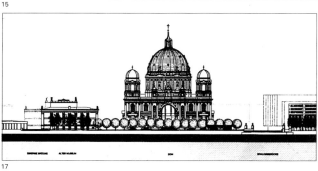

17

92

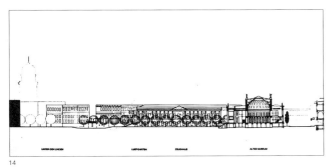

14

16. Proposed project

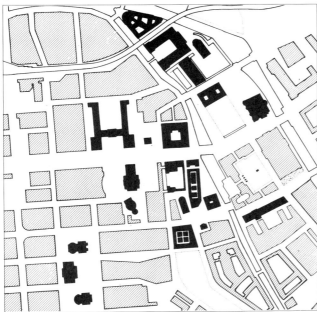

16

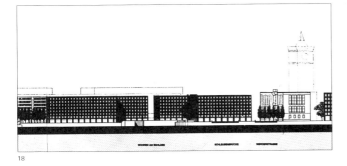

18

19. View from the Kupfergraben

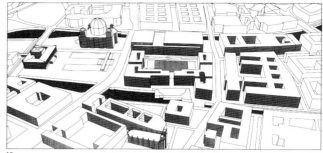

20. Structure of the spaces
21. Structure of the built area

22. First planning stage
23. Second planning stage

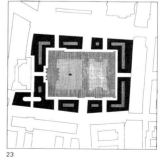

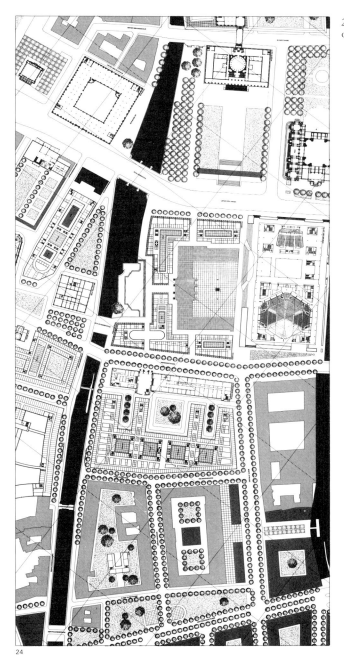

24. Planimetry
of the standard plan

24

STÄDTEBAULICHER IDEENWETTBEWERB

FÜR DEN

DIENSTLEISTUNGSSTANDORT

NEUSS-HAMMFELD II/III

1994
Neuss-Hammfeld

The Neuss-Hammfeld II/III planning area is situated between Neuss old city in the west and the banks of the Rhine and Düsseldorf in the east. To the north it borders on Neuss harbour, to the south on the Hammfeld I industrial estate.

The plan for this new part of the city on the outskirts of Neuss is an exemplary demonstration of the principle of layering. Starting from the form of the planning area, a differentiated, linear urban structure is developed which takes account of the many different requirements: structures for various purposes, existing trees, transport network, spatial structure.

The Four Quadrants

The development area is divided into four quadrants by the intersection of two axes, consisting of the Am Pfauenhof and Hammer Landstrasse streets. These quadrants form the basic structure of the proposed urban development. They differ in terms of their uses and urban character and are therefore treated differently:

– the southwestern quadrant (Hammfeld II): a very variable urban block structure (50 × 100 metres) for the largely undeveloped area, constructed round a central park

– the southeastern quadrant: the plan is based on the slab-like structure of the existing buildings by the Rhine park centre. It is continued along Stresemannstrasse in order to complete the district

– the northeastern quadrant: this quadrant is marked by large-scale structures (wholesale flower market, sewage plant), which divide it into three areas. In the two eastern areas, the existing buildings are supplemented in line with the existing structure. New buildings are constructed in the area near the future Willy-Brandt-Ring, carefully following the course of that street

– the northwestern quadrant (Hammfeld III): much of this land is already built on. The buildings are very heterogeneous and follow no urban planning system. As a means of responding better to this situation, a relatively small-scale block grid is proposed here (50 × 50 metres). The blocks are again grouped around a park.

Superimposed Layers

In a further planning stage, the basic structure established in these four quadrants is differentiated by superimposing the existing structures:

– superimposing the existing buildings: the existing buildings in the competition area are for the most part integrated in the new plan to ensure that it can be carried out smoothly

– superimposing the existing green areas: especially in the Hammfeld II district, the green areas, some of them valuable, are retained

– superimposing the roads: Dehrendorfer Weg and a

crossroad that is appearing beside the riding stable are incorporated in the plan and form the main axes of the network of pedestrian paths.

The superimposition of what already exists on to the basic structure produces the definitive outlines of the blocks.

Block Typology

The typology of the block buildings is determined by their uses. A wide variety of types is possible, but they must satisfy two requirements: first, the development of the land must follow the contours of the blocks and, secondly, the height of the buildings up to the eaves must be a standard c. 25 metres. This ensures that the typology of the buildings and the street areas acquire an unequivocally urban character.

In line with the project specifications, the plan for Hammfeld II/III is mainly for office buildings. At the same time provision is made for other facilities, such as a cinema complex, a hotel and a musical theatre, to enhance the urban quality of the district: these special facilities are sited at significant urban points, for instance overlooking the park (hotel, musical theatre) and on the corner of the Willy-Brandt-Ring and Stresemannstrasse (cinema complex). There should also be some residential buildings, inspite of the problem of their proximity to the harbour, since the boulevard and the central park offer good facilities. In addition, cafés and shops are sited in the arcades along the boulevard.

The specific types of building are based on their various functions: e.g. a block consisting of a single volume (cinema complex), a perimeter block (hous-

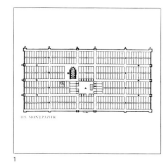

1

2

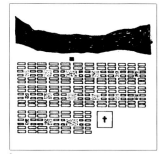

3

Analogous urban structures

1. Montpazier
2. Cordoba
3. Savannah

99

ing), a terraced block (offices), etc. The sizes of the buildings can be varied by combining or separating them.

The New District

The four quarters acquire a decidedly urban character through the height and compactness of the blocks and the precision and proportions of the street areas: a new district thus emerges, linked to Neuss old city by Hammer Landstrasse. Accordingly, it is proposed to extend that street into a spacious boulevard leading from the old city to the banks of the Rhine and finally to a footbridge over the Rhine.

This main axis of the district is framed by two highrise buildings at either end, forming gateways to the old city and to the Rhine. Other highrise buildings are proposed for the centre of the Hammfeld III district: four angled buildings form a *castrum*, which gives this smaller area a clear identity of its own.

Together with the planned Neuss tower, the gateways and the *castrum* form a complex of striking buildings that clearly demarcate the new district in the landscape of the Rhine.

Structures that influence form

4. Existing buildings
5. Existing green spaces
6. Existing roads

101

7. View from the east

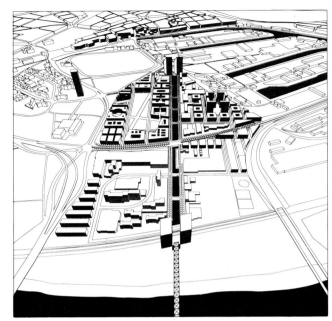

8. View from the south

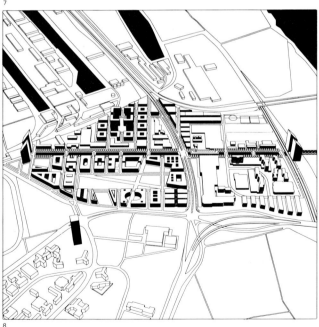

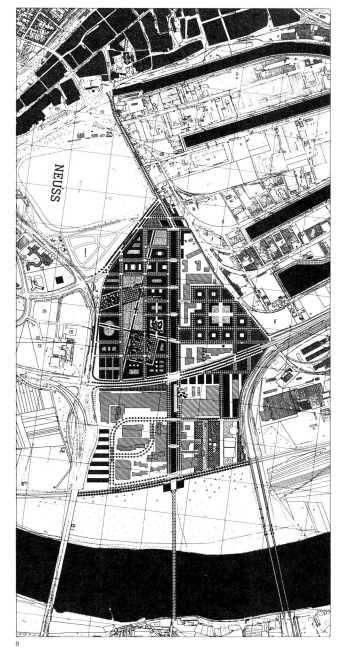

NEUSS

9

10. The development area
10a. Superimposition of the development area with the existing axes to form four quadrants
10b. The four quadrants define the specific structure of the blocks
10c. Existing buildings
10d. Existing green areas
10e. Existing roads
10f. Superimposition of the basic structure on to the existing buildings
10g. Superimposition of the existing green areas
10h. Superimposition of the existing roads
10i. Superimposition of the block structure with the functional requirements

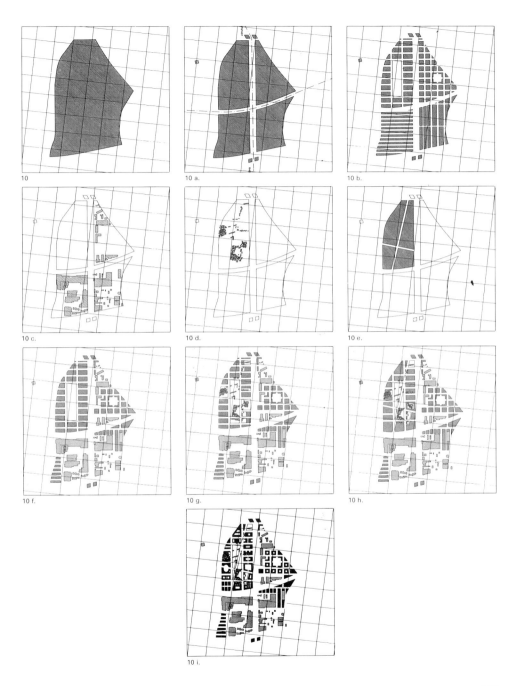

10

10 a.

10 b.

10 c.

10 d.

10 e.

10 f.

10 g.

10 h.

10 i.

11. First planning stage

11

12. Second planning stage

12

13. Third planning stage

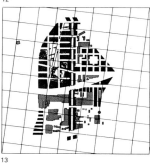

13

14. Fourth planning stage

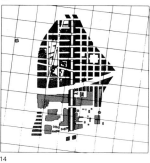

14

15

1991
Potsdamer Platz and Leipziger Platz, Berlin

Like Spreeinsel, the area round Potsdamer Platz and Leipziger Platz reflects the history of Berlin in the 20th century in almost exemplary form. In the twenties, the two squares formed the busiest traffic junction in the Berlin metropolis, after which it turned into a battlefield and eventually into a mined no-man's land. During the postwar reconstruction period, the ruins left over from the war fell victim to a planning whose ideal of the city as a landscaped area was reflected in the adjacent cultural forum, and which deliberately denied the big-city tradition of these squares. Today, the spectator sees a place without history, an urban desert devoid of all rational coherence.

Against this background, the project for Potsdamer Platz and Leipziger Platz sets two objectives: first, the need to define a clear, unequivocally urban place again, with rigorously demarcated spaces and a precisely structured geometry. This also means taking into consideration the historical dimension of the area and restoring the historical continuity of these squares. Secondly, a flexible and rational urban structure is needed, which takes account of the practical requirements of the contemporary city.

Starting from the strategy of the "city as layer," the following plan was proposed:

Urban Structures

Within the planning area, there are various urban structures of some importance. Firstly there is the historical block grid of Friedrichstadt, with its buildings typical of that system, and the dominating, strictly geometrical Leipziger Platz.

Secondly, there are the original parcels of built-up land outside Friedrichstadt, whose network of coordinates still produces an urban effect.

Thirdly, there is the network of streets and transport routes created after the war between Kemper Platz and Leipziger Platz, which has in effect altered the relationship between the different areas.

The new plan is based on consideration for these historical structures.

Superimposed Layers

The superimposition of the block structures of Friedrichstrasse with the present-day road and transport network and the further superimposition of a uniform grid of highrise buildings based on the historical coordinates of the former parcels of built-up land by the zoo creates a dense, structurally complex and differentiated network of streets and blocks of very varied size, form and meaning, which takes account both of the existing proportions of the sites and of their very varied functional requirements.

Block and Street Structure

The differentiated block and street structure produces

a maximum of flexibility in relation both to buildings and to open spaces. The variety of block sizes and forms, ranging from regular street blocks to double blocks, ribbon developments and individual houses, also allows for a wide range of urban designs and architectural forms.

The same applies to the open spaces. Every conceivable type of urban open space is possible, ranging from the central park to smaller squares, streets, avenues (former Potsdamer Strasse), boulevards, pedestrian precincts and arcades, to traffic axes and imposing squares and parks (Potsdamer Platz and Leipziger Platz).

Typologies
The plan is a dense network of superimposed urban layers and building types. A number of basic types can be defined:

– block types: square block, H-shaped block, irregular block, block within a block, denticulate block, composite block

– street types: urban street, traffic street, avenue, boulevard, pedestrian street, passage, gallery

– types of square: ornamental square, four-sided square, eight-sided square, triangular square, irregular square, street square, inner courtyard

– types of highrise building: tower in a park, tower in a block, tower with a base, layered tower, double tower

– types of green space: central park, wide avenue, hedged area, monumental tree, grid of trees, "poché" park.

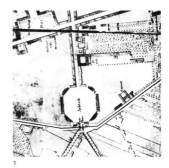

Historical development of Potsdamer Platz and Leipziger Platz 1

1. 1804
2. 1867
3. 1915

Functional Structure

A wide variety of different purposes can be fulfilled within an urban structure that contains a wealth of variants. The individual house (Weinhaus Huth on the former Potsdamer Strasse), the historical building (Esplanade), the superblock used mainly for offices or the multi-purpose block are all an integral part of the general urban structure.

Rules

There is no fixed architectural form or vocabulary. The architectural forms are subjective, depend on the project in question and allow for great individual freedom in the choice of material and style.

As a rule, 22 metres is the highest block height and 180 metres the highest tower height. The grid and height of the tower are binding, the outer form and material are not. The towers are like uniform footprints in the dense network of the blocks. The conflict between tower structure and block structure is intentional and produces the accidental effect that is needed in a complex plan.

Art

Art forms part of the urban design rather than being a decorative trimming. The superimposition of layers can produce a number of larger or smaller residual areas, which are no longer useful to the architect. It is at this borderline between useful and useless space that art comes into its own and uses its own methods to continue the architectural and urban plan in extreme situations, with exaggerated or understated forms.

The accidental situations this creates are characteristic of open spaces that contain sculptures, individual objects, borders and corners. Architecture, urban design and function, history and reality must be seen as a complex unity.

Historical development of Potsdamer Platz and Leipziger Platz 2

4. 1955
5. 1963
6. 1991

7. View from the north-east

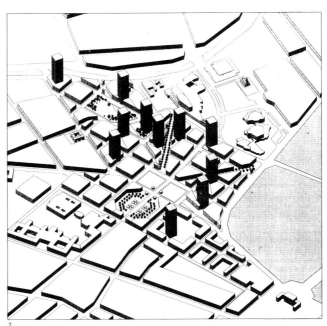

8. View from the east

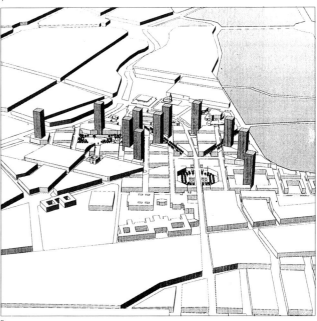

114

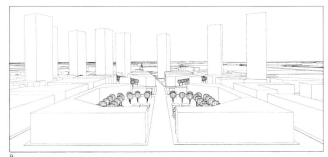

9. View from the Leipziger Strasse

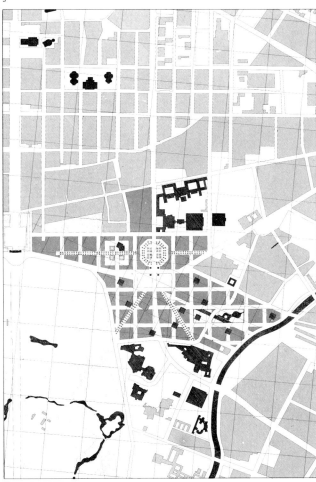

10. General planimetry

115

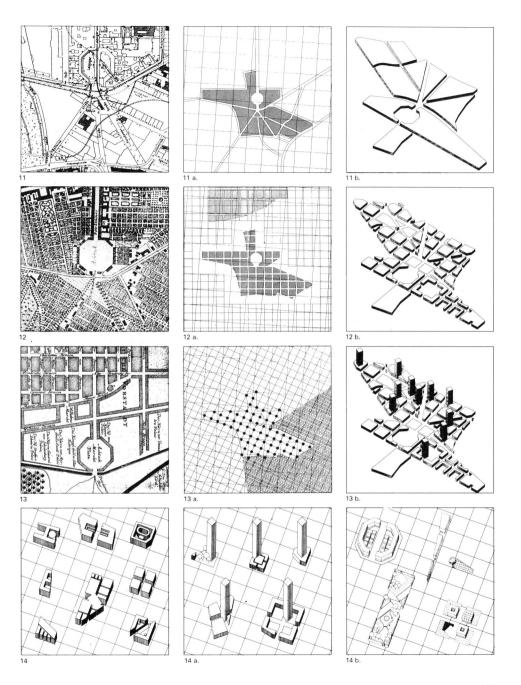

11   11 a.   11 b.

12   12 a.   12 b.

13   13 a.   13 b.

14   14 a.   14 b.

117

15. View from the central park

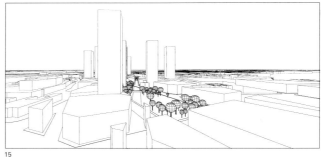

17. Planimetry
of the ground floor

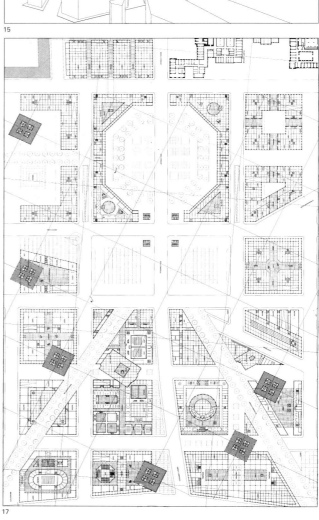

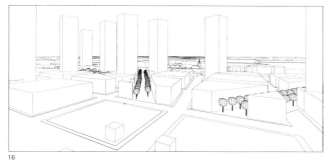

16

16. View of Potsdamer Platz

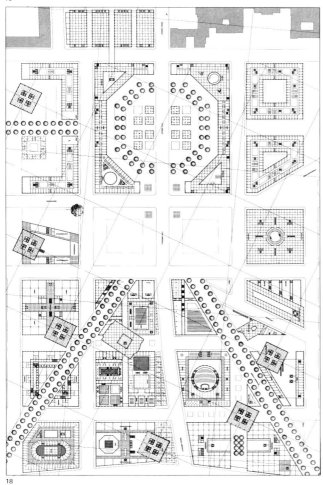

18

18. Planimetry
of the standard plan